Gifts from the Kitchen

Gifts from the Kitchen

LOVE
FOOD

This edition published in 2009

Love Food ® is an imprint of Parragon Books Ltd

Parragon
Queen Street House
4 Queen Street
Bath, BA1 1HE, UK

Copyright © Parragon Books Ltd 2007

Love Food ® and the accompanying heart device are a trademark of Parragon Books Ltd

ISBN 978-1-4075-7901-6

Printed in China

Produced by the Buenavista Studio s.l.
Text by Ann Kleinberg
Photography by Günter Beer
Home economy by Stevan Paul
Design by Cammaert & Eberhardt

Notes for the reader

This book uses imperial, metric, and U.S. cup measurements. Follow the same units of measurement throughout; do not mix imperial with metric.

All spoon measurements are level, teaspoons are assumed to be 5 ml, and tablespoons are assumed to be 15 ml. Unless otherwise stated, milk is assumed to be whole, eggs and individual vegetables are medium, and pepper is freshly ground black pepper.

Recipes using raw or very lightly cooked eggs should be avoided by infants, the elderly, pregnant women, convalescents, and anyone with a chronic condition. The times given are an approximate guide only.

All canning jars must be sterilized before use. Previously used bottles should be scrubbed clean before use. All food gifts should be labeled with the date of preparation.

All food gifts contained inside this book may be stored in an airtight container for one month, unless otherwise stated.

The recipe on page 52 was created with veterinary advice and was tested on various dogs. However, it may not be suitable for all types of dogs and you may need to check (before using the recipe) with your own vet as to its suitability for your dog. The author and publisher of this book cannot be held liable in the case of any allergic reactions suffered by your dog to the recipe itself or any of the ingredients.

Contents

Introduction

Think back to the gifts you have received – which was your favorite and most memorable? Which one put a smile on your face and touched your heart? Most probably it was something made especially for you. The one-of-a-kind present that did not come from the store but was created just for you by a loved one.

That is what *Gifts from the Kitchen* is all about; showing you care for someone with a homemade present they will treasure – and enjoy eating! What could be a more considerate gift than a beautifully packaged box of homemade **Butter Cookies**? What says "Get Well Soon" better than yummy **Chocolate Fudge**? What do you bring to a hostess who tells you, "don't go out and buy me anything – I have everything I need"? Wouldn't you love to dazzle her with a jar of **Brandied Cherries**?

In today's world of mass markets and unbridled consumerism, isn't it nice to take a step back – to a gentler age when friends showed up with a jar of homemade jam or a freshly baked coffee cake? They did not run to the mall to buy a box of chocolates – they made their own. And that effort, of sharing something created in their own kitchen, meant so much. Making your own edible gift is the perfect way to show you went the extra mile – you exerted effort because you really care.

Making and packaging your own edible gifts also gives you a chance to show off your culinary skills. You probably have a specialty or two that you are very proud of. Why not share it with family and friends? Instead of a bottle of wine for a summer picnic, how about surprising your friends with your homemade **Gazpacho**? Or for a Saturday lunch get-together on a cold, rainy day – wouldn't a jar of **Winter Fruit Compote** be perfect?

These homemade gifts offer the perfect solution for that hard-to-please person. For the man who has everything – how about a batch of **Peanut Butter Cream Cheese Brownies** to make him happy? And for that favorite aunt who always brought you candy when you were little? You could return the favor with **Spiced Orange Marmalade** in a jar tied with her favorite color ribbon – just to show you remember.

This collection of edible gifts offers ideas for delicious dishes and wonderful packaging. Try one the next time you are searching for the perfect gift – you will be a star among friends and family. Just remember to make some extra for yourself!

Sweet Treats

Who doesn't love chocolate or candy? It is a rare person who can resist the temptation of a **Chocolate Nut Cluster** or a piece of **Chocolate Fudge**.

When invited to your next dinner party, rather than buy a box of expensive **Chocolate Truffles** from the gourmet retailer in the next town, why not make your own? Present them, each one with different coating, on a lovely white tray and you have made a spectacular gift for a very lucky friend. Feel like being a bit exotic? Nothing could be more unique than box of **Coconut Date Balls** or **Pistachio Turkish Delight**. Put them in an ornate box or place them on a brightly colored dish and you will definitely be thought of as the most original (and favorite) gift giver.

You cannot go wrong with any of the sweet treats presented in this book. While you are at it, be creative and come up with colorful, elegant packaging to wrap up your culinary wonders. Use ribbons, raffia ties, boxes, cartons, jars, canisters, candy dishes—something you have in the house or something you can pick up locally. Do not forget to add your own personal label. The idea is that whatever the packaging, an edible gift that you made yourself is a delightful, imaginative, and very original gift.

Chocolate Nut Clusters

1 cup chocolate chips

1 tbsp unsalted butter

1 cup mixed nuts: peanuts, cashews, almonds, etc.

Makes about 24

Individually wrapped Chocolate Nut Clusters presented on a wooden tray make a very elegant and delicious gift.

Melt the chocolate and butter together in a microwave or over a double boiler. Stir in the nuts.

Drop, a teaspoonful at a time, onto a baking sheet or into little paper cases. Chill until set. Store in an airtight container for up to one month.

Easy Nut Brittle

1 tbsp unsalted butter, plus
extra for greasing

1 cup sugar

$^1/_2$ cup light corn syrup

1 $^1/_2$ cups roasted, salted peanuts

1 tsp vanilla extract

1 tsp baking soda

Makes about 1 lb/450 g

What could be sweeter than piling up a stack of nut brittle and tying it with a gingham ribbon?

Grease a large baking tray and a wide spatula and set aside.

Combine the sugar and corn syrup in a microwave-safe bowl or measuring cup. Microwave on high for four minutes. Remove from the microwave, stir in the remaining butter and the peanuts, return to the microwave and heat on high for another three to five minutes. The mixture should become thick and bubbly and turn a golden pale brown color. Remove from the microwave carefully—it will be very hot. If not using a microwave, combine the sugar, corn syrup, and peanuts in heavy saucepan and stir over a medium heat until the sugar dissolves. Increase the heat to high and boil for about 20 minutes until a candy thermometer registers 295ºF/145ºC, stirring frequently.

Stir in the vanilla and baking soda; the mixture will foam up. Pour immediately onto the greased baking sheet and use the spatula to flatten the mixture out as thinly as possible.

When completely cooled and hardened, break into pieces and store in an airtight container for up to one week.

Chocolate-Dipped Fruit

8 oz/225 g semisweet chocolate
pieces

1 lb/450 g assorted fruit:
strawberries, bananas, dried
apricots

Makes about 1 lb/450 g

Fill up a pretty jar with this chocolate-dipped fruit, attach skewers with a
ribbon, and you have the makings of a great gift.

Melt the chocolate in the top of a double boiler over simmering, not boiling,
water.

Using a toothpick or very thin skewer, spear the fruit, dip it into the
chocolate, hold aloft to allow the excess chocolate to drip back into the pot
and place on a tray covered in parchment paper. Remove the skewer or
toothpick. Continue like this until you have used up all the fruit or chocolate.

Place the tray in the refrigerator uncovered and allow the chocolate to
harden. Serve a platter of chocolate-dipped fruit as is or with pound cake
and a bowl of whipped cream. Store in a refrigerator and consume within two
days.

Chocolate Lollipops

1 cup bittersweet chocolate pieces

1 cup milk chocolate pieces

vegetable oil for spraying the molds

$^1/_2$ cup chopped nuts

Makes 10 to 15 lollipops

Individually wrapped chocolate lollipops are not just for kids – adult chocolate-lovers will go mad for them too.

Melt the chocolate in the top of a double boiler over simmering, not boiling, water.

Pour half the chocolate into prepared lollipop molds that have been lightly sprayed with a vegetable cooking spray. Add the nuts to the remainder of the chocolate, mix well, and fill the remaining molds.

Insert the lollipop sticks into the molds, pushing them in just enough to secure but not all the way to the top.

If using plastic molds or cookie cutters, spread out the chocolate into a $^1/_2$ - inch/1 $^1/_2$ - cm rectangle on top of some parchment paper. Press with the cutter mold and lift off (spraying the inside of the mold with a vegetable spray may help to release the chocolate). Insert the stick. The chocolate lollipops can be stored in a refrigerator in an airtight container for one week.

Chocolate Truffles

2 cups semisweet chocolate pieces

$^1/_2$ cup unsalted butter

1 $^2/_3$ cups heavy cream

1 tbsp vanilla extract

coconut, cocoa, confectioners' sugar, and chopped nuts for coating

Makes 40 to 50 truffles

Is there a more classic treat to go with an espresso than chocolate truffles? Served on a simple white tray, or in a tissue-lined gift box, they are perfection!

Combine the chocolate, butter, and heavy cream in the top of a double boiler over simmering water and stir continuously. Stir in the vanilla, mix well, and pour into a shallow pan. Cover and chill for at least one hour.

Once the chocolate mixture has set, remove from the refrigerator and, working quickly, form small balls out of the chocolate by scooping it out with a melon ball scoop. Roll around in whatever coating you like – coconut, confectioners' sugar, chopped nuts, etc. Place on a baking sheet lined with parchment paper, cover, and chill until ready to serve. The chocolate truffles can be stored in a refrigerator in an airtight container for one week.

Chocolate Fudge

1 cup cocoa powder

$1/2$ cup granulated sugar

1 $3/4$ lbs/800 g sweetened condensed milk

1 cup unsalted butter

$3/4$ cup coarsely chopped nuts (walnuts, pecans)

1 $1/2$ tsp vanilla extract

Makes about 2 $3/4$ lbs/1 $1/3$ kg

Chocolate fudge is such a great treat, as it hardly needs any special packaging. Pile it up, wrap with some raffia and it'll be ready to give away!

Prepare a 9-inch/22-cm square baking sheet by lining it with aluminum foil. Allow the extra foil to extend over the edges of the pan.

Stir together the cocoa and sugar in a heavy saucepan. Add the sweetened condensed milk and the butter and bring to a boil over medium heat, stirring constantly. Continue cooking for ten minutes, stirring frequently. The mixture will be very thick.

Remove the pan from the heat and stir in the nuts and vanilla. Pour into the prepared pan and spread out evenly with the back of a large spoon. Chill for at least four hours or until set. Remove from the refrigerator and use the extra foil from the sides to lift out the fudge. Cut the fudge into 1 $1/2$ x 1 $1/2$-inch/4 x 4-cm squares. Cover and store in the refrigerator. Store in an airtight container for one month.

Pistachio Turkish Delight

vegetable oil, for greasing

4 $\frac{1}{2}$ cups water

4 cups granulated sugar

1 tsp lemon juice

1 cup cornstarch, plus $\frac{1}{4}$ cup for coating

1 tsp cream of tartar

2 tsp vanilla extract

$\frac{1}{2}$ cup chopped pistachio nuts

$\frac{3}{4}$ cup confectioners' sugar

Makes about 2 lbs/900g

These exotic treats should be presented on a brightly colored serving plate or inside a gift box.

Grease a 9-inch/22-cm square baking pan. Stir 1 $\frac{1}{2}$ cups of the water, the sugar, and lemon juice in a saucepan over low heat until the sugar dissolves Bring to a boil, and when it reaches 240ºF/115 ºC remove from the heat and set aside.

Combine 1 cup of the cornstarch, the cream of tartar, and one cup of water in a saucepan but do not heat. Bring the remaining two cups of water to a boil and slowly pour into the saucepan with the cornstarch mixture. Stir well. Turn on the heat and bring to a simmer, whisking constantly as the mixture thickens.

Pour the sugar and lemon syrup into the cornstarch mixture, continuing to stir. Bring to a boil and simmer for 1-1 $\frac{1}{4}$ hours. Stir frequently. It should turn a pale golden color. Stir in the vanilla extract and nuts and remove from the heat. Pour into the prepared baking pan and spread out evenly. Let stand uncovered overnight until it sets.

Combine the confectioners' sugar and the remaining cornstarch and spread out on a board. Cut the Turkish delight into 1-inch/ 2 $\frac{1}{2}$-cm shapes using an oiled knife. Roll each piece in the sugar and cornstarch mixture until it is coated on all sides.

Store in a sealed container with the remaining sugar and cornstarch mixture sprinkled between the layers.

Almond and Cashew Toffee

1 ¼ cups unsalted butter

1 cup granulated sugar

½ cup packed brown sugar

⅓ cup water

1 tbsp light molasses

½ tsp salt

2 cups chopped toasted almonds and cashews

Makes about 2 lbs/900 g

Wrap these toffees in their own paper cases and line them up in a colorful box.

In a heavy saucepan, melt the butter over low heat. Stir in the granulated sugar, brown sugar, water, molasses, and salt and continue to stir until the sugars dissolve.

Increase the heat and bring to a boil, stirring slowly and constantly. Make sure to scrape the bottom of the pan. Continue until a candy thermometer inserted into the pan registers 290°F/145°C. Remove the pan from the heat.

Stir in 225 g/8 oz of the chopped nuts and immediately pour the mixture into the paper cases. Sprinkle with the remaining nuts and chill, uncovered, until firm.

Remove the paper cases from the refrigerator. Store between layers of baking paper in an airtight container, at room temperature or chilled, for up to 1 week.

Coconut Date Balls

1 cup granulated sugar

$^1/_2$ cup unsalted butter

1 large egg, slightly beaten

8 oz/225 g dates, pitted and chopped

2 cups puffed rice cereal

$^1/_2$ cup chopped pecans

$^1/_2$ cup flaked coconut, plus extra for coating

Makes 40 to 50

These elegant and delicious treats should be piled into a box, lovingly wrapped with tissue paper, and covered until ready to eat.

In a saucepan over a medium heat, combine the sugar, butter, egg, and dates. Stir frequently and cook until the dates soften and the mixture thickens.

Remove from the heat, immerse the pan in ice water to cool it down quickly, and add the cereal, pecans, and coconut to the mixture. When cool enough to handle, shape the mixture into small balls, roll in the remaining coconut, and spread out on a serving platter or place between layers of parchment paper in an airtight container for one week.

Chocolate Fondue

2 cups semisweet chocolate pieces

1 cup evaporated milk

$^1/_2$ cup mini-marshmallows

Makes about 3 cups

What fun for young and old – put all the makings for a chocolate fondue together in a box, add colorful napkins, treats, and sticks for dipping, and you have created the perfect dessert gift.

Combine all the ingredients in a heavy saucepan over low heat. Stir until smooth, then remove from the heat.

Transfer to a fondue pot and serve with cubes of pound cake, strawberries, bananas, oranges, marshmallows, or any other appropriate fruits.

Baked Goodies

The appeal of a baked treat, be it a cookie or cake, sweet or savory, is universal and utterly irresistible. What can beat a freshly baked **Coffee Cake** to warm one's heart, or **Chocolate Chip Cupcakes** to delight the child in all of us? Certainly no store-bought item can come close.

Have you been invited to dinner but run out of ideas for what to bring? Why not show up with a gift-wrapped shoe box lined with colorful napkins and filled to the brim with **Cheese Straws**, fresh from the oven?

For an afternoon tea party, there could not be a more perfect gift than a tin of freshly baked **Butter Cookies**. Or combine them with cardboard containers of **Buttermilk Cookies** all tied up with pretty satin ribbons.

If the host has a four-legged friend you could do no better than a dish of homemade **Dog Biscuits**. One taste and you have won over both dog and owner for life!

As with all edible gifts, keep in mind proper packaging. Cakes, cookies, and muffins should first be covered in plastic wrap to preserve them, and then gift-wrapped. Tins and cookie jars make excellent containers. Add a label with a personal note, and do not forget to date it.

Butter Cookies

1 1/2 cups unsalted butter, plus extra for greasing

2 1/2 cups all-purpose flour

2 1/2 tsp baking powder

1/4 tsp salt

1/2 cup granulated sugar

1 tsp vanilla extract

pecan halves, chocolate disks, and/or chopped nuts, for decorating

Makes about 40 cookies

A tin of homemade butter cookies is about as special a gift as it gets!

Preheat the oven to 350°F/175°C. Grease two baking sheets and line with parchment paper.

Combine all the ingredients except those for decoration in a food processor, and process until smooth using a steel blade. Transfer to bowl.

Using a teaspoon, form small balls out of the batter and drop onto the prepared baking sheets, placing them 1 inch/2 1/2 cm apart. To create a variety of cookies, press into them a selection of pecan halves, chocolate disks, and chopped nuts. Place on the center rack of the oven and bake for 20 minutes or until golden brown.

Remove the trays from the oven and set them on a wire rack to cool. Store the cookies in an airtight container for one month.

Peanut Butter Cream Cheese Brownies

6 oz/170 g cream cheese, at room temperature

$^1/_2$ cup peanut butter (creamy or crunchy)

2 $^1/_8$ cups sugar

4 large eggs

$^1/_8$ cup milk

1 cup unsalted butter

1 $^1/_2$ tsp vanilla extract

$^3/_4$ cup cocoa powder

1 $^1/_4$ cups all-purpose flour

$^1/_2$ tsp baking powder

$^1/_2$ tsp salt

1 cup semisweet chocolate chips or pieces

Makes about 36 brownies

Wrap these delicious brownies individually and watch them disappear!

Preheat the oven to 350°F/175°C. Grease a 13 x 9-inch/32 x 22-cm baking pan.

In an electric mixer, beat together the cream cheese, peanut butter, $^1/_8$ cup of sugar, one egg, and the milk. This will make the peanut butter topping for the cake.

To make the brownie mixture, melt the butter and put in a large bowl. Add the remaining two cups of sugar and the vanilla extract. Add the remaining three eggs, one at a time, mixing well with a spoon after each addition. Add the cocoa and mix well. Add the flour, baking powder, and salt, stirring constantly to combine all the ingredients. Stir in the chocolate pieces.

Remove and set aside one cup of the brownie mixture. Pour the remaining mixture into the prepared baking pan and smooth out.

Pour the peanut butter topping over the brownie mixture and distribute it evenly over the top. Using a teaspoon, drop the reserved brownie mixture over the peanut butter topping. Using a fork, spread the two toppings in a wavy motion, swirling together to create a marbled effect.

Bake for 30-40 minutes or until a cake tester comes out clean. Cool on a wire rack. When it reaches room temperature, cut into squares, and remove to a serving plate or store covered in the refrigerator.

Corn Muffins

1 cup milk

¹/₂ cup vegetable oil

2 eggs, lightly beaten

2 tbsp unsalted butter, melted

2 tbsp honey

1 tsp vanilla extract

1 ¹/₄ cups all-purpose flour

³/₄ cup yellow cornmeal

¹/₄ cup sugar

1 tbsp baking powder

¹/₂ tsp salt

cornflakes (optional)

Makes 9 large or 12 medium muffins

Corn muffins make the perfect breakfast, snack, or anytime treat. Present them in individual paper cases.

Preheat the oven to 400°F/200°C. Grease a muffin pan and add paper cases for easy removal.

Beat together the milk, oil, eggs, butter, honey, and vanilla extract.

In a separate bowl combine the flour, cornmeal, sugar, baking powder, and salt. Make a well in the dry ingredients, add the wet mixture, and stir just enough to combine – do not over-stir.

Spoon the batter into the prepared paper cases, and bake for 15-20 minutes or until a cake tester comes out clean. Remove the muffin pan from the oven and cool on a wire rack for at least five minutes before removing the muffins from the pan. Store in an airtight container at room temperature. These muffins may be frozen.

For an extra-special kick, add ¹/₃ cup of cornflakes into the mixture. What a crunchy surprise!

Vanilla Cake with Cinnamon Streusel Topping

1 1/2 cups all-purpose flour

1 1/2 tsp baking powder

1 cup granulated sugar

1/2 cup unsalted butter, melted and cooled, plus extra for greasing

1/4 cup milk

2 large eggs

1/2 tsp vanilla extract

1/3 cup brown sugar

2 tsp cinnamon

1/4 cup unsalted butter, at room temperature, cut into small cubes

1/3 cup chopped pecans

Makes 1 loaf cake

Give the whole cake or perhaps just a few individually wrapped slices—each with its own fork!

Preheat the oven to 350°F/175°C. Grease a 9 x 5-inch/22 x 12-cm loaf pan.

Sift together the flour and baking powder.

In an electric mixer or food processor, cream the sugar and 1/2 cup melted and cooled butter. Add the flour mixture, then the milk, eggs, and vanilla extract. Mix well and pour into the prepared loaf pan.

Combine the brown sugar and cinnamon. Using a pastry cutter or fork, cut in the 1/4 cup cubed butter pieces and the pecan pieces. Mix to just combine. Distribute chunks of the cinnamon and pecan mixture over the batter.

Bake for 40 minutes or until a cake tester comes out clean. Remove and cool for ten minutes on a wire rack. Loosen the sides of the cake from the pan, give the pan a few taps, and slip the cake out of the pan onto a plate. Reverse onto a wire rack and continue to cool. Once cooled, store in an airtight container for up to one month.

Chocolate Chip Cupcakes

³/₄ cup unsalted butter,
plus extra for greasing

1 cup granulated sugar

3 large eggs

1 tsp vanilla extract

³/₄ cup all-purpose flour

³/₄ cup cocoa powder

¹/₂ tsp baking powder

¹/₄ tsp salt

¹/₂ cup buttermilk

¹/₄ cup chocolate chips

Makes 12 cupcakes

These cupcakes make the perfect gift for any chocolate lover. Present them in individual paper cases in a pretty box tied with matching ribbons.

Preheat the oven to 350°F/175°C. Prepare a 12-cup muffin pan by greasing and adding paper cases.

In an electric mixer, cream the butter and sugar until light and fluffy. Add the eggs, one at a time, beating well after each addition. Beat in the vanilla extract.

Sift together the flour, cocoa, baking powder, and salt. Add the flour mixture and buttermilk alternately to the mixing bowl, starting and ending with flour. Stir in the chocolate chips by hand.

Pour the mixed batter into the prepared cups, filling each about ³/₄ full. Bake for about 20 minutes or until a cake tester comes out clean. Cool in the pan for 5–10 minutes, then remove from the muffin pan and cool completely on a wire rack. Once cooled, store in an airtight container for up to one month.

Cheese Straws

½ cup unsalted butter, softened, plus extra for greasing

8 oz/225 g sharp Cheddar cheese, grated

4 oz/100 g Parmesan cheese, grated

1 cup sifted all-purpose flour

½ tsp Worcestershire sauce

Serves 6

What a fun thing to bring to a party. Put them in individual glasses, provide pretty napkins, and let the festivities begin!

Cream the butter in an electric mixer, then add the remaining ingredients. Turn onto a lightly floured work surface and shape the dough into a ball. Cover with plastic wrap and chill for several hours.

When ready to bake, preheat the oven to 425°F/220°C.

Divide the dough into 1-inch/2 ½-cm balls. Roll each ball into a long thin strip, like a straw. Place on a lightly greased baking sheet on the center rack in the preheated oven, and bake for 10-12 minutes, or until golden and crispy. Once cooled, store in an airtight container for up to one month.

Buttermilk Cookies

2 cups all-purpose flour

1 tbsp baking powder

1 tsp granulated sugar

$^1/_2$ tsp salt

5 tbsp unsalted butter, cold, cut into small cubes, plus extra for greasing

$^3/_4$ cup buttermilk

semisweet chocolate, for decorating (optional)

Makes about 8 cookies

What wonderful surprises can be hidden inside take-out cartons!

Preheat the oven to 425°F/220°C. Grease a baking sheet.

In a large bowl, combine the flour, baking powder, sugar, and salt. Cut in the butter cubes using a pastry cutter or fork. The mixture should have the consistency of coarse crumbs.

Add the buttermilk to the flour mixture and stir until well blended. Transfer to a lightly floured work surface and knead the dough for 30 seconds. Shape it into a $^3/_4$ inch/2 cm thick rectangle.

Using a 2 $^1/_2$–3-inch/6-7-cm cookie cutter, cut out circles of dough, and place them at least 1 inch/2 $^1/_2$ cm apart on the baking sheet. If you do not have a cookie cutter, drop mounds of dough onto the baking sheet using a tablespoon.

Bake on the center rack of the oven for about 12-15 minutes, until puffed up and golden. Remove the tray from the oven and let stand for five minutes. Transfer the cookies to a wire rack to cool completely.

These cookies are great served as they are or with Strawberry Butter (page 74). You can also melt semisweet chocolate and drizzle a bit onto the cookies for an extra sweet treat. Once cooled, store in an airtight container for up to one month.

Madeleines

2 large eggs

$^2/_3$ cup granulated sugar

1 tsp vanilla extract

$^1/_2$ tsp grated lemon peel

pinch of salt

1 cup all-purpose flour

10 tablespoons unsalted butter, melted and cooled, plus extra for greasing

confectioners' sugar, for decorating (optional)

Makes 18 madeleines

Any way you present this classic French treat will be wonderful. Why not in its own tray with a brightly colored placemat and matching ribbons?

Preheat the oven to 375°F/190°C. Butter and flour two 9-hole madeleine pans (little shell-shaped indentations) or use the same pan twice.

In an electric mixer, beat the eggs and granulated sugar until creamy. Add the vanilla extract, lemon peel, and salt. Slowly add in the flour and beat until just blended. Gradually add in the cooled butter in a steady stream and mix in.

Spoon one tablespoon of the mixture into each cup, filling it $^3/_4$ full. Place on the center rack of the preheated oven and bake for about 15–20 minutes or until a cake tester comes out clean and the madeleines are puffed up and golden. Remove to a wire rack to cool and then drop the madeleines out of the pan onto a serving plate. Dust with confectioners' sugar, if using, and serve.

Irish Soda Bread

³/₄ cup currants

2 cups all-purpose flour

1 ¹/₂ tsp baking powder

¹/₂ tsp baking soda

2 tbsp granulated sugar

¹/₂ tsp salt

4 tbsp unsalted butter, chilled
and cut into cubes, plus extra for
greasing

1 large egg, beaten

²/₃ cup buttermilk

¹/₈ cup milk, for brushing

Makes 1 loaf

You do not have to be Irish to love this bread. Present the whole loaf as a
wonderful Sunday brunch gift.

Preheat the oven to 375°F/190°C. Grease the bottom and sides of an 8-inch/
20-cm loaf pan, and place a layer of greased parchment paper inside. Dust
with flour. Plump up the currants by soaking them in warm water for several
minutes.

Sift together the flour, baking powder, baking soda, sugar, and salt. Cut in
the chilled butter using a pastry cutter or fork. The mixture should have the
consistency of coarse cornmeal.

Add the drained currants to the flour mixture. Beat together the egg and
buttermilk and add to the mixture, stirring well. Turn out onto a lightly
floured work surface and knead briefly. Place into the prepared cake pan.
Brush the top with milk and place on the center rack of the oven.

Bake for 35-40 minutes. Remove from
the oven and let cool for several minutes.
Transfer to a wire rack, let cool completely,
then flip out and invert back onto a serving
plate. Cut into slices.

Banana Bread

2 cups all-purpose flour

1 tsp baking powder

$3/4$ tsp baking soda

$1/2$ tsp salt

2 medium eggs

1 cup granulated sugar

$1/2$ cup vegetable oil, plus extra for greasing

1 tsp vanilla extract

2 cups mashed bananas (3-4)

$1/2$ cup yogurt

Makes 1 loaf

No one can resist banana bread. Wrap it in a pretty napkin, tie it with a ribbon, and find a loaf pan to give it away in.

Preheat the oven to 350°F/175°C. Grease a 9 x 5-inch/22 x 12-cm loaf pan.

Sift together the flour, baking powder, baking soda, and salt. Set aside.

In an electric mixer, cream the eggs and sugar. Add the oil and vanilla extract and mix well. Mix in the mashed bananas.

Add the flour mixture alternating with the yogurt, starting and ending with the flour. Pour into the loaf pan, place on the center rack of a preheated oven, and bake for about one hour or until a cake tester comes out clean. Remove from the oven and let stand for ten minutes. Turn out of the loaf pan, invert onto a wire rack, and let cool completely. Once cooled, store in an airtight container for up to one month.

Dog Biscuits

2 $\frac{1}{2}$ cups whole wheat flour

$\frac{1}{2}$ cup powdered milk

$\frac{1}{2}$ tsp garlic powder

1 tbsp wheat germ

2 tsp beef bouillon powder

$\frac{1}{3}$ cup vegetable oil or bacon grease

1 large egg

$\frac{1}{2}$ cup ice water

Makes about 24 cookies

Fido will love this treat made just for him. Fill his bowl with these cookies and you will have made a friend for life.

Preheat the oven to 350°F/175°C. Lightly grease a baking sheet.

In a large mixing bowl, combine the flour, powdered milk, garlic powder, wheat germ, and beef bouillon powder. Add the oil and egg, and stir well. Mix in the ice water one tablespoon at a time, just until the mixture comes together.

Turn out the mixture onto a lightly floured work surface and roll out to $\frac{1}{2}$ inch/ 1 $\frac{1}{4}$ cm thickness. Cut out cookies using a cookie cutter and place on the greased baking sheet 1 inch/2 $\frac{1}{2}$ cm apart. Place on the center rack of the oven and bake for 25 to 30 minutes or until firm. Remove from the oven and cool completely.

For a firmer texture, leave the cookies in the oven after they have finished baking, but turn off the heat and leave the oven door open a crack. Once cooled, store in an airtight container for up to one month.

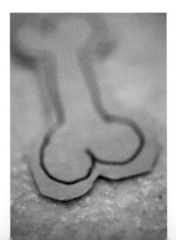

Preserves and Condiments

Sure you can call your local store and have them send your cousins some fancy jam for the holidays. But wouldn't a jar or two of your own **Candied Orange Peels** mean so much more? Send it along with a recipe for your favorite fruitcake and you have created a gift that is unique, delicious, and unforgettable.

Yes, a case of wine for a friend's housewarming would be lovely. But wouldn't a set of beautifully bottled **Honey Dijon Mustard**, **Herbs de Provence Oil**, and **Spicy Olives** make a really special statement? Place the individually labeled bottles in a wooden box, snuggle them in with confetti or colored tissue paper, and write a personal message on the outside with a homemade label. If you have a computer, you can whip up labels in no time.

When you are invited over to friends' for Sunday brunch, if muffins, scones, or even plain old toast are on the menu, you can turn delicious into divine with a ramekin or two of your homemade **Strawberry Butter**.

While you are thinking about what to make, remember that stylish packaging is essential and adds that special touch. Just keep in mind that canning jars should be sterilized before use, previously used bottles should be scrubbed clean, and food gifts should always be labeled with the date of preparation. Add a recipe that goes with the food or perhaps a lovely dish to serve it in and you will be known as the perfect gift giver!

spiced Orange Marmalade

¹/₃ cup sugar

¹/₄ cup brandy

2 sticks cinnamon

2 whole star anise

1 tsp vanilla extract

2 tbsp grated orange peel

5 whole cloves

one 16-oz jar orange marmalade

Makes about 2 cups

Add marmalade to a jar, seal, wrap it with a piece of linen, and tie it all up with a pretty bow.

In a heavy saucepan over a medium heat, combine all the ingredients except the marmalade and bring to a simmer. Continue to cook until the mixture is reduced.

Add the marmalade and bring to a simmer. Remove from the heat, let cool, and store refrigerated in sealed jars.

Candied Orange Peels

3 large oranges

2 lemons, halved

3 cups water

2 cups granulated sugar, plus more for coating

$^{1}/_{4}$ cup Cointreau or Grand Marnier liqueur (optional)

Makes about 2 cups

Why not present these candied orange peels in their own glass box?

This recipe involves blanching the peels three separate times and then boiling them in sugar syrup.

Using a sharp knife, cut the peels off the oranges taking care to get rid of all the white pith. Cut into very narrow similar-size strips, and then cut in half lengthwise. Place all the peels and half a lemon into a saucepan. Add water to cover, bring to a boil, and boil the peels for 15 seconds. Drain immediately, rinse with cold water, and drain again. Repeat this entire process two more times.

In another saucepan, bring the three cups of water and two cups of sugar to a boil. Cook until the sugar has totally dissolved, then add the orange peels that have been blanched three times and the remaining lemon half. Bring to a boil and simmer gently for 15 minutes.

Remove the saucepan from the heat, add the liqueur if desired and leave as is, loosely covered overnight.

Remove the peels from the saucepan and lay them out individually on parchment paper. Toss the granulated sugar over the peels and roll them around in the sugar to totally coat them. Let dry. Store the sugared peels in an airtight container. They may be dipped in melted semisweet chocolate for an extra-special treat.

Brandied Cherries

1 lb/450 g fresh cherries

1 cup brandy

$^3/_4$ cup granulated sugar

$^3/_4$ cup water

1 tbsp lemon juice

Makes about 4 cups

A jar of these homemade brandied cherries will delight any recipient, but remember, these need to be made one month in advance.

Snip off the stems of the cherries, leaving $^1/_2$ inch/1 $^1/_2$ cm. Rinse the cherries in cold water. Place in a heatproof jar and cover with brandy (make sure that the jar is large enough to accommodate more liquid). Cover the jar, but do not seal it. Leave out for several hours, preferably overnight.

In a heavy saucepan over medium heat bring the sugar, water, and lemon juice to a boil and simmer for ten minutes. Pour the brandy from the cherry jar into the saucepan and stir in. Once blended, pour all the liquid over the cherries in the jar(s) and seal.

Allow to stand for one month before use.

Winter Fruit Compote

4 cups water

2 cups sugar

2 sticks cinnamon

10 black peppercorns

one 1-inch/2 $1/2$-cm piece fresh ginger

grated zest of 1 lemon

grated zest of $1/2$ orange

2 tsp vanilla extract (or 1 vanilla bean)

4 apples

4 pears

2 cups pitted prunes

1 cup dried apricots

Serves 8 to 12

A ceramic pitcher is the perfect way to present this yummy edible gift.

In large, heavy saucepan over medium heat bring the water and sugar to a boil. Add the next six ingredients, bring to a boil, lower the heat, and simmer for ten minutes.

Peel and core the apples and pears, and cut into quarters or eighths. Add to the saucepan and cook until just softened (about five minutes). Do not overcook the fruit. Add the prunes and apricots, cook for an additional five minutes, and remove from the heat.

Let the mixture cool and pour into prepared jars. Store chilled.

spicy olives

2 lbs/900 g Kalamata olives

1 lemon

1 fresh red hot chile pepper

2 cloves garlic, sliced

5 sprigs thyme

$^1/_2$ cup olive oil, or more

salt and pepper

Makes about 4 jars

If a glass jar was filled with these olives and accompanied by some wooden cocktail sticks, people would start picking immediately!

This recipe is great for spicing up any type of olive, but Kalamata are especially good.

Cut the lemon into quarters, then cut each quarter across, creating small chunks. Leave the chile pepper as is, or slice it thinly for a spicier mix (make sure to protect your hands and DO NOT touch your eyes!).

Mix all the ingredients together, place in decorative jars, and let marinate for several days before use. The flavor just improves over time. Keep refrigerated and bring to room temperature before eating (the coagulated oil needs time to become liquid again).

Onion Jam

2 lbs/900 g red onions (or white)

6 tbsp butter

$1/4$ cup granulated sugar

$1/2$ cup red wine vinegar

1 cup dry or semi-dry white wine

salt and pepper

Makes about 2 cups

A sealable jar with a screw-top lid is all you need to present this delicious onion jam.

Cut the onions in half and slice each half into very thin slices.

Heat the butter in a large skillet over high heat, add the onions, and when they start to turn translucent, add the sugar. Lower the heat to medium and cook covered for 20 minutes, stirring occasionally.

Add the vinegar and white wine and bring to a simmer. Add salt and pepper to taste and cook uncovered for about one hour. The mixture should reduce and take on a jam-like texture. Taste and season to individual preference.

Pickled Radishes

2 cups sliced radishes

2 small red onions, thinly sliced

$^1/_2$ cup white wine vinegar

$^1/_2$ cup granulated sugar

2 tsp salt (or to taste)

5 whole black peppercorns

Makes 2 cups

Go Asian with this dish by presenting it in little dishes on a wooden tray.

Combine the radish and onion slices in a large jar.

Combine the vinegar and sugar in a saucepan over low heat and stir until the sugar dissolves. Combine with the salt and peppercorns, mix well, and pour over the radishes and onions. Cover the jar and chill at least overnight for best flavor.

Pineapple Corn Relish

1 cup corn kernels (fresh or frozen)

1 cup fresh or canned pineapple chunks

$1/2$ red onion, coarsely chopped

1 small red hot chile pepper (optional), finely minced

$1/3$ cup fresh chopped cilantro leaves

2 tbsp olive oil

2 tbsp cider vinegar

1 tbsp honey

salt and pepper

Makes about 2 $1/2$ cups

Fill a bowl or jar with this relish, cover, and offer with serving spoons.

If using fresh corn, prepare by either steaming in a microwave or quickly sautéing in a hot skillet.

Combine the corn with the pineapple, onion, chile pepper, and cilantro in a bowl. Make a marinade out of the remaining ingredients, mix well, and pour over the pineapple and corn mixture. Toss together. Chill, covered, and let marinate several hours before use.

Honey Dijon Mustard

1 ³/₄ cups dry mustard powder

³/₄ cup water

¹/₂ small onion, minced

1 ³/₄ cups dry white wine

¹/₃ cup white wine vinegar

2 tsp sugar

1 tsp salt

5 cloves garlic, crushed

1 whole bay leaf

1 tsp whole allspice

³/₄ cup honey

Makes about 2 ¹/₂ cups

Nothing would be more appropriate for this gift than to present it in a clay jar tied with a lovely ribbon.

Stir the mustard powder and water together to form a paste. Put in a medium bowl.

In a heavy saucepan over medium heat combine all the remaining ingredients except for the honey, bring to a boil, then lower the heat and simmer for about 10-15 minutes. The mixture should reduce to half the amount.

Use a strainer to pour the liquid into the bowl with the mustard paste. Stir well until blended, return to the saucepan, and cook over low heat stirring constantly for about five minutes or until the mixture is well blended and thickened. Add the honey, remove from the heat, and stir well. When cooled, pour into clean jars and store chilled.

Strawberry Butter

³/₄ cup unsalted butter

6 ripe strawberries, cored and sliced

1 tbsp granulated sugar

pinch of salt

Makes about 2 cups

This delicious butter will delight any recipient – present it in a little glass jar and watch them smile!

Place all the ingredients in a food processor and using the steel blade, process for one to two minutes or until smooth. Scoop out, transfer to a crock or ramekin, and keep, covered, in the refrigerator.

The Strawberry Butter should be brought to room temperature before serving.

Herbes de Provence Oil

4 sprigs thyme

2 sprigs rosemary

2 sage leaves

1 small lavender sprig

1 ½ cups olive oil

Makes 1 ½ cups

You cannot go wrong with a cruet for this classically flavored oil. It makes a lovely decorative gift – just put all the herbs in an attractive container, add the olive oil, seal, and give it away!

Preheat the oven to 300ºF/150ºC.

Bruise the herbs by crushing them or gently hitting them with a wooden spoon, which helps to release their flavors. Add to a two-cup ovenproof glass measuring cup, then add the oil. Place the measuring cup on a pie plate in the center of the preheated oven. Cook for at least one hour. Remove, let cool, pour into a jar, cover, and refrigerate. The herbs will have roasted so they will no longer be pretty to look at, but they will have added a wonderful flavor to the oil. Leave as is or strain them out.

The oil must be refrigerated to prevent any bacteria from forming.

Raspberry Mint Vinegar

1 $1/_2$ cups fresh mint leaves

3 cups fresh raspberries

2 cups red wine vinegar

$1/_4$ cup granulated sugar

mint sprigs, to garnish

Makes 2 cups

Find a lovely jar, fill it with this vinegar, and tie on a few sprigs of mint to make a wonderful gift.

Rinse and dry the mint leaves. Bruise them by gently hitting them with the back of a wooden spoon (this releases their flavor).

Pick over the raspberries and mash them with a fork.

Place the vinegar and sugar in a stainless steel pan and bring to a boil over medium heat. Lower the heat to simmer, add the mint leaves and raspberries and simmer for five minutes. Remove from the heat and let cool.

When cooled, pour into a glass jar, cover, and store in a dark place until the taste is to your liking. Strain the vinegar through a sieve (discarding the solids) and pour into a decorative container. Add fresh mint sprigs for decoration and store covered.

Mango Chutney

2 large mangoes, peeled and cubed

2 large tart apples, peeled, cored, and chopped

1 small red onion

$1/2$ medium sweet red bell pepper, chopped

$1/2$ cup golden raisins

$1\,1/2$ tbsp grated fresh ginger

1 cup granulated sugar

$1/2$ cup white wine vinegar

1 tbsp lemon juice

$1/2$ tsp each: turmeric, nutmeg powder, cinnamon, cloves, and salt

pepper to taste

Makes 2 cups

Fill up a canning jar with this wonderful chutney and give it to someone with a sweat tooth.

Combine all the ingredients up to the lemon juice in a heavy stainless steel or enamel saucepan and bring to a boil over high heat. Reduce the heat and simmer uncovered for 20 minutes or until the fruit is tender and the mixture is softened. Stir occasionally.

Add the lemon juice and all the spices and cook for an additional five minutes.

Remove from the heat and let cool. Pour the chutney into jars, cover, and refrigerate. It can be kept for one to two weeks.

On the Table

The nicest words a hostess can hear are, "what can I bring?" And even though she may answer, "nothing at all," she would probably be very grateful if you persisted. Bringing a present of food says, "let me help – I appreciate your invitation and I'd love to participate."

In this chapter we present ideas for starters and main course additions, foods that can go directly onto the table. What better way to start off a meal than with **Gazpacho** laced with a shot of ouzo? How about offering to bring jars of your own **Tomato** and **Pesto Sauces** and join your friends in a pasta-making party?

For the quintessential way to enjoy good times in a casual setting, there is nothing like an outdoor barbecue. Rustle up some steaks, open some good bottles of wine, and bring over a jar of your "secret" **Barbecue Sauce**.

Any of these gifts can be (and should be!) beautifully packaged in canning jars, attractive bottles, or decorative dishes. Check your pantry – you probably saved some wonderful decorative containers because you just could not part with them. Now you can put them to good use by filling them with your own homemade specialties. Add a label with your name and the date on it, tie a pretty ribbon around the jar, and you are in business!

Gazpacho

$^{1}/_{2}$ onion, sliced

2 cloves garlic

3 tbsp olive oil

$^{1}/_{4}$ cup red wine vinegar

5 large tomatoes, coarsely chopped

1 large cucumber, peeled and coarsely chopped

1 medium green bell pepper, coarsely chopped

$^{1}/_{3}$ cup chopped fresh cilantro leaves, plus extra to garnish

2 tbsp tomato paste

dash Tabasco sauce

tomato juice (optional)

Serves about 6

This gazpacho is a perfect way to start a summer meal. Add a bottle of ouzo or anise-flavored liqueur to go with it and this gift will be a huge hit!

Add all the ingredients to a food processor bowl and process until a chunky purée forms. You may have to do it in more than one batch. For a smoother soup, keep processing. For a thinner soup, add some tomato juice.

The soup is best if prepared in advance and chilled for several hours before serving.

It may be served with a few drops of ouzo drizzled on top and chopped cilantro leaves dropped in the center of the soup when it is ladled out.

spicy Nuts

1 cup shelled whole almonds

1 cup pecan halves

$^1/_2$ tsp chili powder

$^1/_2$ tsp ground cumin

$^1/_2$ tsp curry powder

$^1/_2$ tsp cinnamon

$^1/_2$ tsp garlic salt

$^1/_2$ tsp black pepper

2 tbsp olive oil

coarse salt or garlic salt
(optional), to garnish

Makes about 2 cups

Fill up a cellophane bag with these nuts, tie a ribbon or two around it, and you have created a great present.

Preheat the oven to 325°F/165°C.

Combine the nuts in a bowl; set aside.

Mix the spices together. Heat the oil in a skillet over a low heat and add the spices. Stir for a few minutes until the flavors are well combined. Remove from the heat and add to the bowl of nuts. Toss well.

Cover a baking sheet with aluminum foil and spread out the spiced nuts in a single layer. Bake for 15 minutes, stirring them once or twice. Remove from the oven, toss, sprinkle with coarse salt or garlic salt, if using, and let cool. Once brought to room temperature, they can be stored in a sealed jar for one month.

Tomato Basil sauce

2 lbs/900 g ripe tomatoes

2 tbsp olive oil

1 large onion, finely chopped

2 tbsp tomato paste

1 bay leaf

8 fresh basil leaves,
or 1 $^1/_2$ tsp dried

1 tsp sugar

salt and pepper

Makes about 2 $^1/_2$ cups

Give a jar of this homemade sauce to any pasta lover you know and they will never forget it.

Blanch the tomatoes in a pot of boiling water for a few seconds to loosen the skin. Remove from the water with a slotted spoon and peel off the skins. Coarsely chop the tomatoes.

In a heavy saucepan, heat the oil over medium heat. Add the onions and sauté until golden. Add the tomatoes, tomato paste, bay leaf, basil leaves, sugar, and salt and pepper to taste.

Bring to a boil, reduce the heat, and gently simmer uncovered for about 45 minutes, stirring occasionally. Remove the bay leaf, let cool, and store in sealed jars in the refrigerator for one week.

Pesto Sauce

4 cups fresh basil leaves

$1/_3$ cup pine nuts

3 cloves garlic

$1/_2$ cup olive oil

$1/_2$ cup Parmesan cheese

$1/_2$ tsp salt, or to taste

Makes about 1 cup

Fill up a canning jar with this pesto sauce, add a wooden spoon, tie it all together with a colorful ribbon, and what a wonderful gift!

Add the basil leaves, pine nuts, and garlic to a food processor and process. With the motor running, slowly add a stream of olive oil until a paste is formed.

Scrape down the sides of the bowl, add the cheese, and process until smooth. Transfer to a bowl; add salt to taste and store refrigerated in sealed jars for one week.

Barbecue sauce

3 tbsp olive oil

1 large onion, finely chopped

3 cloves garlic, crushed

1 cup white vinegar

$^3/_4$ cup ketchup

$^1/_3$ cup apple juice

$^1/_4$ cup firmly packed dark brown sugar

2 tbsp Dijon mustard

2 tbsp Worcestershire sauce

1 tsp salt

1 tbsp Tabasco sauce

1 tsp cayenne pepper, or to taste

$^1/_2$ tsp chili powder

Makes about 1 $^1/_2$ cups

There is nothing like a canning jar to say "homemade." Add a label that you printed yourself and you are in business!

Heat the oil in a skillet, add the onion, and sauté. Add the garlic and cook until golden.

Add the remaining ingredients, bring to a boil over medium heat, reduce the heat, and simmer for 15-20 minutes. Stir occasionally.

Store in a sealed jar and refrigerate. This sauce will keep for about a week.

Cheese Fondue

³/₄ cup dry white wine

1 tbsp cornstarch

2 tsp water

1 clove garlic, crushed

8 oz/225 g Emmental cheese, coarsely grated

8 oz/225 g Gruyère cheese, coarsely grated (or use Cheddar)

salt and pepper

French bread, apples, pears, and vegetables for dipping

Serves 6

For a wonderful present, combine cheese, garlic, dipping forks, a few plates, and a fondue pot, and put it all in a beautifully wrapped box.

Add the wine to a heavy saucepan and bring just to a simmer.

Disolve the cornstarch in the water and add to the saucepan. Add the garlic. Gradually add the cheese to the pan while stirring, being careful not to let it ball up. Add salt and pepper to taste.

Bring the contents of the pan to a simmer and cook for six to eight minutes. Transfer to a fondue pot set over a flame. Serve with cubes of French bread, apple and pear slices, and raw vegetables.

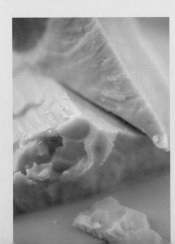

Index